JUNETEENTH

BY VAUNDA MICHEAUX NELSON
AND DREW NELSON

ILLUSTRATIONS BY
MARK SCHRODER

On My Own
HOLIDAYS

M Millbrook Press/Minneapolis

Thanks to Shannon Barefield, Kitty Creswell, Tracey Adams, Kris Sporcic, Lori Snyder, Stephanie Farrow, Lucy Hampson, and Katherine Hauth.   —V.M.N. & D.N.

Millbrook Press
A division of Lerner Publishing Group
241 First Avenue North
Minneapolis, MN 55401 U.S.A.

Website address: www.lernerbooks.com

Library of Congress Cataloging-in-Publication Data

Nelson, Vaunda Micheaux.
    Juneteenth / by Vaunda Micheaux Nelson and Drew Nelson ; illustrations by Mark Schroder.
      p.   cm. — (On my own holidays)
   ISBN-13: 978–1–57505–876–4 (lib. bdg. : alk. paper)
   ISBN-10: 1–57505–876–6 (lib. bdg. : alk. paper)
    1. Juneteenth—Juvenile literature. 2. Slaves—Emancipation—Texas —Juvenile literature. 3. Slaves—Emancipation—United States—Juvenile literature. 4. African Americans—Social life and customs—Juvenile literature. I. Nelson, Drew, 1952–. II. Schroder, Mark, ill. III. Title. IV. Series.
E185.93.T4N45 2006
394.263—dc22   2005015334

Manufactured in the United States of America
1 2 3 4 5 6 – JR – 11 10 09 08 07 06

For the sisters: Olive, Willa, Laura, Rene, and Charlotte
—V.M.N.

For Christyl and Justin
—D.N.

For my wife, Nicole
—M.S.

Jubilee!

It is June 19th, 1865,

a hot day in Texas.

Clouds decorate the bright blue sky.

On a farm outside the city of Galveston,

a man hoes corn.

Five miles away,

a teenage boy chops wood.

Nearby, a woman scrubs the floor.

Her sister milks a cow in the barn.

It seems like a normal day.

Then a message arrives in Galveston.

It races from ear to ear through town.

The message is carried

to the countryside

by riders on horseback.

It is carried by wagon

and by people on foot.

The people on foot are running

because the message

is so important.

When the news reaches
the man in the cornfield,
tears roll down his cheeks.
Five miles away, the young woodcutter
plants his ax in a stump
and runs to hug his father.

Nearby, the woman stops scrubbing
and dances across the wet floor.
Her sister drops a bucket of milk
and falls to her knees.
As the news spreads across Texas,
people stop working and jump for joy.

These men, women, and children
were not ordinary workers.

They were black slaves.

The news that arrived on June 19th
changed their lives forever.

On that day, General Gordon Granger
arrived in Galveston.

He read an order from
President Abraham Lincoln.

The order said that the slaves were free.

This was good news,
but it was old news.
President Lincoln had given
the order in 1863.
But slaves in some places
were not told right away.
It took more than two years
for the order to reach Texas slaves.
When it finally did,
the streets of Galveston rang
with black voices shouting,
"We're free! Free! Free!"

Slavery

But how did black people
become slaves?
Imagine that you are playing outside.

Suddenly, you are captured in a net
like an animal.
You are packed in the bottom of a ship
with many other stolen people.
You are taken far away
to another country.
You are forced to stand naked
on a platform called an auction block.
A man pays money for you.
He owns you now.
You are his slave.
You must do everything he says,
and he can do whatever he wants to you.
He can make you work.
He can put chains on you.
He can whip you, even kill you.
You never again see your
home or your family.

Beginning in 1619, these things happened
to millions of African people.
They were taken to North America
and to other places as slaves.
Why did Americans want slaves?
Some people in the North wanted
housekeepers and farmhands.
Many Southerners needed people
to work on their plantations.

Plantations were huge farms for cotton,
tobacco, corn, and other crops.
Plantation owners sold these crops
to make money.
The owners could keep more money
if they did not have to pay
the people who worked for them.
They did not pay slaves.

War, 1861–1865

Not everyone wanted slavery.
Many people in the North
and some in the South
wanted to free the slaves.
They knew that slavery was wrong,
and they spoke against it.
They believed that all people
are created equal.

Most Southerners did not want slavery to end.
Without slaves, who would pick their crops
and chop their wood?
Who would cook their meals
and clean their houses?
Also, many white people believed
they were better than black people.
They believed that blacks were *not* equal,
so slaves did not deserve to be free.

Northern leaders would not give up,
and the Southern states would not give in.
Finally, a group of Southern states
decided that they could no longer
be a part of the United States.
They broke away and formed
the Confederate States of America.

Now the country was divided into two parts,
the Confederacy in the South
and the Union in the North.
On April 12, 1861,
armies from the two sides
began to fight.
This was the start of the Civil War.

Freedom

On January 1, 1863, President Lincoln
signed a special order called
the Emancipation Proclamation.
It said that slaves in the Confederate states
were "forever free."
Many plantation owners
did not tell their slaves
about President Lincoln's order.
They wanted the slaves to keep working.

Even when the owners knew that
the South would lose the war,
they wanted one more free harvest.
But Union soldiers brought the news
to slaves as the troops
moved through the South.
Those slaves spread the word to others.
Thousands of freed slaves joined
the Union army to help win the war.

Some Texas slaves heard tales about
freedom, but they couldn't be sure
these stories were true.
Slaves had to be careful.
If they even *talked* about freedom,
their owners might punish them.
Slaves who tried to leave the plantations
would be whipped or killed.
All they could do was wait and hope.

Finally, in April 1865,
the Union won the Civil War.
More than 700,000 people from the North
and the South had died fighting in this war.
On June 19th, Union General Granger
brought the news of freedom
to Galveston.
Texas was the last state where
the official announcement was made.

Slaves No More

Not everyone believed the announcement.

More than 200 years had passed

since Africans were first captured

and brought to North America.

By 1865, most slaves in North America

had been born here.

The only life they knew was slavery.

Then, in an instant, they were free!

Once slaves knew the truth,

they stopped working.

The moment was scary and wonderful.

They were free!

They laughed and cried,

shouted and prayed.

They danced and sang,

gathered and hugged.

They imagined their lives as free Americans.

Some former slaves left the plantations
with just the clothes on their backs.
They didn't know where they were going.
They were happy just to be free to go—
anywhere.
Many searched for loved ones
who had been sold to other plantations.
Some were reunited with their families.
Others never found their parents or children.

Some former slaves found jobs in cities.
Others could not because white people
wouldn't hire them.
Many stayed on plantations
because they had nowhere else to go.
The slaves were free,
but black Americans would struggle
for equal rights for a long time.
Still, the end of slavery brought great joy
and a reason to celebrate.

Juneteenth

On June 19, 1866, one year after
they had learned of their freedom,
former slaves came together to celebrate.
The city of Galveston was
alive with music.
The sweet, smoky smell
of barbecue filled the air.

Black Texans were wearing
their Sunday best.
They gathered and hugged.
They shared news and told stories.
They sang spirituals celebrating freedom.

"No more slavery chains for me.
No more, no more."
Folks attended ceremonies,
worship services, and parades
to mark the day.

This was the first of many
June 19th celebrations in Texas.
And when black Texans
moved to other states,
they took the tradition with them.
But how did June 19th
become *Juneteenth*?
At first, Texans called it Freedom Day,
Emancipation Day, Jubilee,
or simply June 19th.
As years passed, and freedom's
stories were told and retold,
June and *19th* blurred together
into *Juneteenth*.

Today, Juneteenth is celebrated
much like that first anniversary in 1866.
People of all colors arrive
at parks, churches, schools,
and backyards for picnics.
The sweet, smoky smell
of barbecue fills the air.

Potato salad, corn on the cob, biscuits,
homemade ice cream, cakes, pies,
and melons crowd the tables.
Red velvet cake and red soda pop
are traditional treats.
Red honors all the people whose blood
was shed in slavery and in the
struggle for freedom.

Festive parades fill city streets
with music and dancing.
Black cowboys and cowgirls clop
through town on horses.

Miss Juneteenth waves
from a decorated float.
Folks stroll along, singing songs
of freedom and patriotism.

Spirited baseball games bring whoops and hollers from excited fans. Footraces, sack races, and rodeos spark cheers and laughter.

At the cakewalk, people clap
their hands and tap their feet.
Dancers turn and leap, strut and quick-step
to win the grand prize—a delicious cake!

Worship services and readings
of the Emancipation Proclamation
are important parts of Juneteenth.
Speakers tell and retell stories
of slavery and freedom.
They share tales of why Texas slaves
were last to get the news.
One legend says that the first messenger
sent with the proclamation
was murdered along the way.
Another story says he was given
a very, *very* slow mule to ride.
People laugh, but no one forgets
the real reason for the late news.
No one forgets that Juneteenth is not
just a day to have fun.
It is a time to remember.

Juneteenth is celebrated in big or small ways
almost everywhere in the United States.
The government of Texas made it
a state holiday on January 1, 1980.
From Florida to Alaska,
California to New Jersey,
other states across the nation
have followed this example.

Some people believe that June 19th
should be a national holiday,
like Thanksgiving or the Fourth of July.
Wherever it is celebrated,
Juneteenth is a time to sing praises
for the end of slavery in the United States.

Freedom Days

Americans have different ideas about when to celebrate the end of slavery. Some think it should be January 1, the day that President Lincoln signed the Emancipation Proclamation in 1863. Others feel that December 18, 1865, was the true day. On this date, the Thirteenth Amendment to the United States Constitution became law. This amendment ended slavery in *all* of the states. The Emancipation Proclamation freed slaves only in the Confederate states. And there are people who honor the date when slaves were freed in their own state. Whatever date *you* choose, freedom is worth celebrating.

A Freedom Song
"No More Auction Block"

No more auction block for me,
No more, no more!
No more auction block for me.
Many thousand gone.

No more slavery chains for me,
No more, no more!
No more slavery chains for me.
Many thousand gone.

No more captain's whip for me,
No more, no more!
No more captain's whip for me.
Many thousand gone.

No more auction block!
No more auction block!
No more auction block!
Many thousand gone.

New Words

amendment (uh-MEHND-mehnt): a change to the United States Constitution. The Constitution explains the powers of the government and the rights of the people.

cakewalk: a dance contest with a cake as the prize

civil war (SIH-vuhl WOHR): war between groups of people who live in the same country

emancipation (ee-man-suh-PAY-shun): freedom from slavery

jubilee (JOO-buh-lee): a time of rejoicing, often a special anniversary

patriotism (PAY-tree-uh-tiz-ehm): being proud of one's country

proclamation (prok-luh-MAY-shun): a formal public announcement of important news

red soda pop: cherry or strawberry soft drinks. In early Juneteenth celebrations, people drank fresh lemonade with red food coloring added.

red velvet cake: chocolate cake made with red food coloring

spirituals (SPEER-uh-choo-uhlz): religious folk songs of black Americans